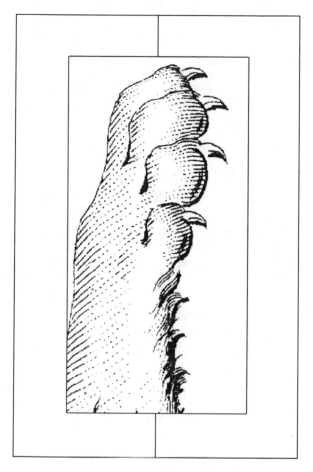

MANAGEMENT COURAGE
HAVING THE HEART OF A LION
MARGARET MORFORD

Cold Tree Press
Nashville, Tennessee

Library of Congress Control Number: 2006928719

Published by Cold Tree Press
Nashville, Tennessee
www.coldtreepress.com

ISBN 1-58385-089 -9

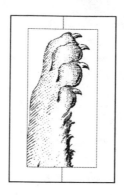

ACKNOWLEDGEMENTS

I owe special thanks to my mother, who never chickened out and wouldn't let us either, who went without so her "girls" could have all the education we needed and thereby all the choices not always available to her.

Thank you to Aunt Peg, who constantly teaches me about being honest *and* kind, and to Unc, who told me he would ask me how this book was coming every time we spoke on the telephone until I finished it. (You'll need a different New Year's resolution for 2007!)

And to Dave, who edited the manuscript, researched publishing options for me, and, in his kindest manner, told me to quit "squandering" the opportunity to be heard. Thank you, Grasshopper!

Most of all, thank you for reading this book. I hope it makes you braver and more satisfied with your work, whatever that may be. Imagine how different work would be if we all had the heart of a lion!

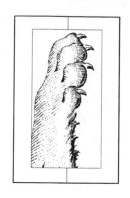

TABLE OF CONTENTS

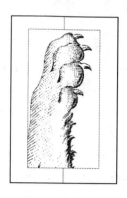

INTRODUCTION

I AM A BUSINESS HERETIC. Many of the strategies recommended in this book are contrary to what we are told by business experts today. The honesty and emotional involvement crucial to Management Courage are diametrically opposed to the "spin" and message-management we get in our daily lives — especially our work lives. It takes real courage to manage against the norm. Management Courage will make you different from your fellow managers. Some days, that will make you feel good about your job. Other days, it will isolate you. But make no mistake. Ultimately, your use of these strategies will pay huge dividends in your professional life. You'll be the type of manager you've dreamed of being — and the kind of manager people dream of working for. So I invite *you* to become a business heretic too, and take your career to a whole new level!

On a personal note, I am humbled by all of you who asked if I had a book you could read — who thought what I had to say was meaningful. Now that the book is alive and kicking, I suspect some may say it is too emotional or too spiritual to be a business book. That's exactly what's wrong with work today. It's not emotional *enough,* or it *wears* on the spirit rather than *feeding* the spirit. Others may say this book contains too many stories about my own career. Yet, if I'm offering examples of failing at Management Courage, whose career could I better use than my own? This book was created for experienced managers who need a resource that encapsulates the highest ideals for which they constantly strive. It also is for young managers who seek principles on which to launch their careers, who do not want to learn by trial and error as most of us have done. Finally, some may say *Management Courage* is too short to be taken seriously. I hope it is short enough that people will read it!

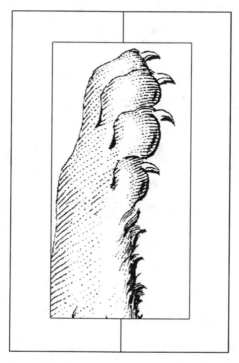

MANAGEMENT COURAGE
HAVING THE HEART OF A LION
MARGARET MORFORD

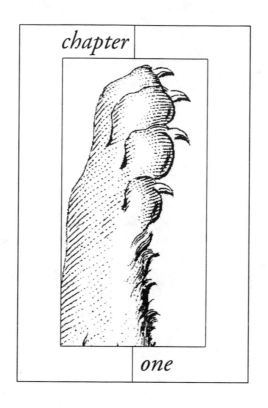

chapter

one

THE FIRST PRINCIPLE:
Be *Painfully* Honest

**"Management Courage requires not just
honesty, but being the most honest you can be
in every situation."**

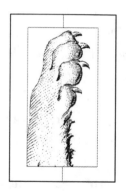

CHAPTER ONE

TODAY'S WORKPLACE IS IN CRISIS. Thanks to absurd "one size fits all" strategies that dangerously lag behind our rapidly changing workplace, managers are demoralized, frustrated, and all too often, parties to conflict.

The result? Far too many workplaces are under-performing and at grave risk of stagnating or going out of business because they will be unable to attract or retain the people needed to lead their organizations forward.

The Revolutionary Solution "Management Courage"

The solution to today's demoralized, unmotivated workplace is a powerful shock therapy I call Management Courage.

What is Management Courage?

First, let me tell you what it *isn't*. It *isn't* about avoiding pain, going through the motions, or doing things "because we've always done it this way," simply so you don't rock the boat.

You know those TV ads for the U.S. Marine Corps? They stress that they DON'T want just anyone to enlist. Rather, they're looking for "a few good men."

Well, Management Courage is a lot like that. It's not for the complacent or faint of heart.

It's for those with the good old-fashioned gumption to choose a harder course of action in the short-term — one that guarantees unpleasant short-term results — so you, your organization, and your employees can profit from a MUCH better result in the long-term.

Why You *Need* to Take "The Road Less Traveled"

In the following chapters, I'll shed clear, powerful light on the six Principles of Management Courage. I'll show you exactly why each is crucial to this revolutionary management action plan, and how each one will help you transform yourself and your employees into passionate, empowered, highly-energized performers who will absolutely maximize your organization's potential.

I'll also show you how you can become the type of manager people WANT to work hard for, one who brings out the absolute best in everyone you supervise and one whom the very best employees refuse to leave, even during the most challenging of circumstances.

Let's face it. Courage is in short supply today. But because it's so rare, it's highly valued — by employers, managers, and employees alike. When I ask people to discuss the most courageous thing they have ever seen a manager do, they speak of these acts with reverence and awe.

Manager's Mantra:

People spend more time at work than anywhere else. They want the experience to be meaningful. They want to work for managers who want to make a *difference.*

Remember — people yearn for more value in their work than their paycheck. This deep-seated need has never been more acute than in today's marketplace. With the recent scandals in corporate America, employees are crying out to work for managers they trust, managers who step up even when it's hard.

How Principle One Led to the Larger Concept of "Management Courage"

The birth of the concept of "Management Courage" came without the proverbial "bang" that normally heralds the beginning of something big. It came from an off-hand remark made in a class I teach called, "Effective Performance Appraisals — The Good, the Bad, and the Ugly." One day, a particularly hostile manager in the class asked, "So tell me . . . How do I motivate my star employee, when all my company allows are 3% raises?"

A deafening silence fell over the class and everyone froze. Before answering, I asked the class members for clarification of their company's raise process. "Do I understand that while you get 3% for raises, you aren't *required* to give everyone 3%? It's actually 3% of your entire annual payroll? And you get to decide how to disperse those monies. Isn't that right?"

Everyone nodded.

So then I asked, "So you actually *could* give a star employee 5%, right? This would be 2% more than the majority of your employees get and would reward the star performer for excellent performance. In addition, it would send a clear message to the rest of your organization about how valuable he or she is to you."

The class confirmed they were allowed to do this, but no one ever did. Why? Because that would mean another employee would only get 1%.

So I asked, "Do any of you have employees who just barely do enough to get by . . . or who only do what you tell them to do — and no more?" Again, practically every manager nodded. "So what do they get as a raise?"

Almost every manager said those employees got 3%, or maybe 2.8%, to make the point that they needed to work harder.

"And does losing just two-tenths of a percent motivate these employees to do better, or do you get the same effort from them year in and year out?" I asked.

All the managers knew the answer, so then I asked, "If you are going to have an employee who will be unhappy with his or her compensation, shouldn't it be your *least productive* employee and not your *star* employee?"

Looking around the room, I saw my point had hit home. But I wasn't quite finished. I needed to put a finer point on it.

"The person who merely does an adequate job year in and year out should be given a raise that keeps him or her current with the cost of living, nothing more. But that doesn't usually happen because we, as managers, lack the Management Courage to be painfully honest with these employees. In this case, we lack the Management Courage to reward our best employees — by giving them 5% raises — because we don't want to have the unpleasant conversation with the employee who will get only 1%."

Manager's Mantra:

When managers lack the courage to be *painfully* honest, everyone in the organization suffers.

A Star (Management Plan) is Born

We moved on through the class, but during the break and afterwards, several managers pulled me aside to tell me what they were doing about raises.

"Do you think I lack Management Courage by doing the following?" they would ask me, before offering details. Then two managers stopped me afterwards and asked me what Management Courage was. They asked if I could give them some examples of Management Courage so they would understand what they must do to demonstrate it.

Because these managers challenged me to articulate what Management Courage was, I began to crystallize my thinking about it, and to look for examples of Management Courage among the managers and executives with whom I worked.

First, I started gathering examples of Management Courage and looking for a common theme. It quickly emerged:

Management Courage is the transforming force
demonstrated when managers choose
a harder course of action *in the short-term* —
one that guarantees unpleasant immediate
results for the manager — so they can create a better result
for the organization and its employees *in the long-term.*

When heroes in emergency or combat situations speak later about their amazing acts, they rarely are aware of how remarkable their choices were. They speak in terms of "doing the right thing" and acting for the greater good.

That's precisely what Management Courage will accomplish for you, your employees, and your workplace.

By exhibiting Management Courage, you can make a genuine difference in the lives of the people with whom you work and the organization for whom you work.

While Congress can require certain business ethics, the bone-deep character of Management Courage cannot be legislated. You must want it, strive for it, and live it — one management act at a time.

Behind-the-Scenes at Your Workplace: Other Examples of Painful Honesty Making a Difference

I tell stories of Management Courage throughout this book because they are illustrations of each of the Principles as they occur in real life. (The names have been changed, but the situations are real.) Each Principle will be illustrated with examples so you can begin to see Management Courage opportunities as they occur in your work life. To further encourage you to practice each Principle, there are thought-provoking Management Courage questions at the end of each chapter. These should help you understand not only what Management Courage is, but how to begin to see opportunities to practice it.

Honesty in the Management Courage context goes beyond the old adage your parents quoted about honesty being the best policy. That adage only requires that everything you say be true, it doesn't require you to do (or be) more than that. But Management Courage honesty is entirely different, in that it requires you to speak *the painful truth* even when you don't have to. However, Management Courage honesty stops short of being cruel or mean. I always recoil from people who say, "I just tell it like it is." Often, I find this to be an excuse to be brutal to another human being — guilt-free. Being the most honest is a balancing act, an art that few managers attain. Those who do engender great loyalty in their employees that others admire but seldom understand.

Most likely, you have been the victim of a lack of

Management Courage honesty at least once in your career. You have probably applied for a job, made it to the short list of candidates, and then not been hired. If you are at all savvy, you call whoever was in charge of the interview process and ask in an artful way why you were not the candidate selected. You will almost always get an honest answer which goes something like this, "We found a better, more qualified candidate." Certainly that's truthful. (Obviously, the other candidate was better or he or she wouldn't have been selected.) But the answer is not particularly *helpful.* Had the person told you one of your answers to a question was weak, or even that you "blew" a question, you could work on that answer and not repeat the mistake in another interview.

Displaying Management Courage During the Job Interview Process

Most people will not be honest about why you weren't selected because the hassle of being that honest is rarely worth the trouble it causes the person you've asked for the feedback. After 25 years in business, I find that if I give candidates honest feedback on why they weren't selected for the position, they want to argue with me about why it wasn't the way the interview panel viewed it, or they make excuses for what they did in the interview process. It becomes a monumental waste of time for me, and the candidate benefits very little. Since becoming a believer in Management Courage, I now step up and am the most honest I can be to help the candidate. However, I preface my remarks by saying that I'm happy to provide feedback, but when I have done this in the past, those requesting the feedback wind up arguing with me about our perceptions in the interview process or about the credentials of the selected candidate. I then ask, "If you're sure you want the feedback, I'll give it to you, but you may find it painful to hear." Sometimes individuals will thank me for my honesty, but not wish to trouble me further, and sometimes they show their own brand of Management Courage and ask what I can share with them. (Which candidates do you think do better in their next interview?)

Real-Life Examples of "Management Courage Honesty" Benefiting Both Employers *and* Employees

An interesting employment law case arose in the Seventh Circuit Court of Appeals in Chicago. An African-American woman, working as a "road maintainer," had repeatedly asked for different work assignments, believing it would advance her career. Her supervisors assigned some of the work she requested to other male employees, who happened to be white. Because she kept getting evasive answers from her supervisors about why the other (male) individuals got these assignments, she concluded her supervisors were biased against her because of her race and gender, and sued her employer. The Court of Appeals finally dismissed the lawsuit — but only after the employer produced much documentation demonstrating that the males were better qualified for the tasks assigned, and after spending a great deal of money defending their managers' decisions.

Why didn't the supervisors simply sit down and talk with the woman about why someone else was selected for these assignments? Because they were afraid they would get sued. But they got sued *anyway!* Although it can't be stated with certainty, being "Management Courage honest" with the woman might have helped the employer avoid a lawsuit and minimize the frustration and bad feelings the employee suffered throughout this process. At a minimum, it would have kept the employer from treating the woman unfairly by never giving her a straight answer as to why she wasn't being offered new assignments.

Two Eye-Opening Experiences from My Own Career

I've had two experiences with Management Courage honesty that had a profound effect on my management style. I joined a manufacturing company as the head of Human Resources. We drew workers from some of the more rural parts of the counties around our plant. The work was hard, hot, and tough, but the employees were good and generous people. I had a staff of five, most of whom had been with the company a number of years. I was very definitely the outsider — city girl with a law degree. One of the people who worked for me was particularly bright, but only had a high school diploma. She was one of the most effective people in Human Resources with whom I have worked. She had been in the same job for years and had never gotten promoted. I quickly figured out why. Her grammar was poor and she sounded uneducated. We were owned by a parent company based in the North, so you can imagine how "simple" they thought she was merely because of the way she spoke.

No one had ever talked with her about her grammar. I admired and depended on her, and knew she was capable of doing more if she was just given the chance. It took me a month or two to work up the nerve to talk with her about her grammar because I liked her so much, valued our relationship greatly, and knew I ran the risk of offending her.

Finally, the moment arrived. I opened the conversation by saying, "Greta Grammar, you think like a professional, you act like a professional, you strategize like a professional, but you don't speak like a professional. Because of this, people have a tendency not to listen to what you have to say. It's also what I believe is holding you back from being promoted. I can help you if you want some help with this." At first she looked like I'd slapped her, but she recovered quickly and said she wanted to improve her grammar so she could be promoted. At that point, I offered to send her to a grammar course, and bought her an easy-to-read, entertaining grammar book.

In true eye-to-eye Greta fashion, she directed an insightful question at me: "How did you learn to talk so good?" she asked. I thought about it and told her my mother had always corrected my grammar. (She still does, by the way!) Greta then asked if I would correct her grammar the same way. We agreed that when it was just the two of us, I would correct any grammatical mistakes she made.

It was a grueling experience for both of us. Some days Greta had a hard time getting through two sentences without my interrupting her to correct her grammar. I can remember at least twice asking her if she wanted to quit doing this.

(A definite lack of Management Courage on my part!) She refused to give up and we continued to work together in private. The result? When I left the company five years later, they promoted Greta into my position.

My second experience with Management Courage honesty came when a woman who worked for me displayed Management Courage in dealing with *me*. Cathy was in the process of hiring an individual to work in the finance area of our company. It was an entry-level position, but the Vice President of the area (Archie) wanted final say in who would join his group. Cathy asked me to talk to Archie about a particular candidate — an odd request because normally she, not me, handled this discussion. I asked her why she didn't simply talk to Archie herself. Instead of making an excuse, she looked me squarely in the eye and said, "Everyone knows and talks about the fact that Archie doesn't like minorities, doesn't like women, and doesn't like fat people. You're only one of those and I'm all three. In addition, his boss is your peer and he will understand you have more power than he does. If you recommend he hire this person, he will do what you ask because he is very politically astute. She's a great candidate — much more qualified than anyone else we've interviewed — and will do an exceptional job. Oh, and by the way, she's an African–American female."

How Archie (Bunker) Saw the Light

I called Archie and, with some urgency, told him I needed to see him as soon as possible. When I entered his office, I shut the door and told him I had something very distressing and painful to share with him. I prefaced what I was about to say by telling him I would expect him to share something like this if he had come by this information about me. I went on to explain that I was going to tell him what people said about him around the company, and that it was going to be hard for him to hear. You can imagine how tense he was at this point. I then said, "People say you don't like working with women, you don't like working with minorities, and you don't like people who are overweight." I wish I could tell you that he had an epiphany at that moment, fell on his knees, and confessed to being a chauvinistic bigot. Instead he got mad, said it wasn't true, and that he wanted it stopped immediately. I reminded him no one can stop the grapevine from saying whatever it wants. I went on to suggest that if his next hire was an African-American female, people would have a hard time continuing to say those things about him. He then asked me if we could find an African–American female candidate for his open position. I presented him with the resume Cathy had given me. I cautioned him that if he hired the candidate, he had to make sure it worked out or it would only make him appear to be even more chauvinistic and prejudiced.

The African-American woman he hired was still with the company (and happy) when I left several years later. Each hire Archie made after that changed the make-up of his department. It only happened because Cathy was "Management Courage honest" with me, and I was painfully honest with Archie.

Unsettling Questions To Test Your Management Courage

1. Of the people I manage (or interact with regularly), with whom have I not been the most honest?

2. Am I preparing the people that work for me for promotion? If not, am I moving them to jobs where they can be promoted?

3. Is there anyone I manage (or interact with regularly) whom I believe is not promotable or is in the wrong job? Have I told them this when we discussed their job or a promotion?

4. Have I ever discussed a suspected drug or alcohol problem with an employee or with a co-worker? Or do I just address their lack of performance and eventually fire them or let them get terminated?

5. Is there anyone I manage (or interact with regularly) who should be coached about a behavior pattern that is impeding his or her professional development?

6. Do I pay people what a job is *worth* or merely the salary for which I think I can hire them?

NOTES

NOTES

NOTES

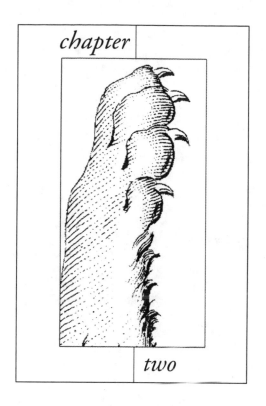

chapter

two

THE SECOND PRINCIPLE:
Never Treat People Identically

**"Management Courage requires that you
treat people equitably, but not identically."**

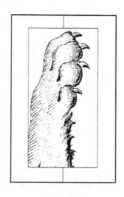

CHAPTER TWO

E VERY MANAGER IS TAUGHT from the moment they enter management that if they treat everyone the same, they can never get into trouble. This has been drilled into all managers because employee lawsuits continue to increase at an alarming rate. Managers cannot be accused of favoritism, or worse, discrimination, if they do the same thing for everyone. While it is an effective way to control risk in an organization, it destroys the motivation of your best employees — the ones who can really make a difference to your organization in the long run.

Smart, hardworking employees resent being treated like everyone else. They see themselves as different from their co-workers and want to be treated as individuals. They want to work for managers who recognize their unique talents and respond to their needs accordingly. When employees make an extra effort to complete a task or go the extra mile for a manager, they have an unspoken expectation that their manager will do the same for them. Sometimes that expectation simply involves permission to leave early in order to take care of some personal business. It flies in the face of human nature to believe good employees will be content with a manager telling them apologetically, "I can't do this for you because I'd have to do it for everyone else."

Of course, good employees can be given the time off, and it doesn't require that the manager allow everyone to leave early. However, it does require a manager to face his or her work group and say, "Joe is leaving early today because he always stays late to finish the last orders." The reason managers aren't open like this is because they know special consideration for one employee generates requests from everyone else for the same thing. It requires strength to say "no" to other employees who never stay late, and to tell them that when they make the effort Joe does, you'll be glad to make the same extra effort for them. Instead, we destroy the motivation of our best employees in order to avoid having uncomfortable conversations with less productive employees.

Manager's Mantra:

It is crucial that the level of employee performance determines the level of reward.

I realize "Never Treat Employees Identically" is high heresy in corporate America today, especially from someone who has practiced law. However, it is crucial to emphasize that the level of performance determines the level of reward. Yes, everyone must have the same opportunities to excel —

I'm not arguing for favoritism or discrimination — but how many of you spend more time with your troubled employees than with your star performers? That's an inequity you need to re-think.

Principle Two in Action

In one of the corporate groups I managed, the employees were equally divided between those with young children and those with grown or no children. When Halloween rolled around, I allowed those with children to leave early to get home and dress their children and take them trick or treating. Everyone else would remain to run the department. Then, at the end of that week, I allowed all of those who had worked on Halloween to leave early and start their weekend, while those with young children would stay to close the office.

As you begin to look at whether you treat everyone equitably (not identically), be aware that there is a growing discontent from employees about the special consideration given to employees with young children versus those without. I have heard numerous employees complain that their co-workers with young children get time off for school plays, first days of school, field trips, etc. and that they are expected to pick up the slack while these employees are away. These people aren't anti-children, but they do feel slighted. You don't get these complaints if managers are plugged in to what is important in each employee's life. For example, managers can allow employees with no children to leave early to start their vacations or to go to a special concert. Giving these employees time off to take their pets to the vet also goes a long way toward resolving these inequities.

Managers don't address these inequities for two reasons. First, they don't know enough about what is important to individual employees to be able to offer each person something of value to him or her. Second, they don't want to have to defend their actions on behalf of one employee to another. It's all a lack of Management Courage.

Sally Sulker Enters the Picture

I had an employee who wanted every possible thing she could get for herself. She had a young child and I gave her plenty of time off to take care of her child's needs. She came to my office on the Friday before she was to start her vacation, dropping hints that she wanted to leave early like some of the other employees had been able to do. I showed a decided lack of Management Courage by ignoring her hints during her first two trips to my office. I knew what she wanted and simply didn't want to argue with her about the fact that I had given her time off for other things. She was a pouter and a sulker, which made me want to avoid this conversation even more. I also found myself contemplating reverting back to the corporate policy, charging everyone leave time and doing nothing special for anyone. It certainly would have saved me an unpleasant discussion with Sally Sulker. But it also would have forced me to abandon one of the important ways

I communicated how much I appreciated extra effort when we needed it.

Finally, on Sally's third visit to my office to remind me she was starting her vacation at 5:00 pm, my Management Courage backbone kicked in. I said to her, "Sally, if all these visits to my office are a subtle (not so subtle in my mind) way of asking if I'll let you go early like I did Jack and Sarah a few months back, the answer is 'no.' In the past few months, I have given you time off for several things you wanted to do with your child. You can't double dip and get both." She told me I didn't understand the importance of being a mother since I didn't have children and began to try to make me feel guilty. I responded by telling her that while I didn't have children, I had recognized how important her role as a mother was by arranging for her to be off when her child had a special event, just as the time I gave Jack and Sarah also was recognition of things that were important in *their* lives. You can imagine the pouting and sulking that took place after our conversation. The rest of Sally's day was filled with very long sighs. Everyone in the department came by at one time or another to ask me what was wrong with Sally. When I told them that I couldn't discuss it, they, of course, went to Sally and asked her. She immediately told them how unfair I was being. However, these were the same coworkers who'd covered for her more times than any one could remember. So my Management Courage garnered me great loyalty from them. They respected the fact that I would face down the unpleasant situation and not ignore it or cave in to it.

Manager's Mantra:

Not treating people identically can actually help create a more positive workplace.

When I first joined that same company, one of the employees came to see me. She told me she had to leave no later than 5:00 pm every day to pick her children up at day care. She also said that while she couldn't stay late, she would come in early in the morning or take work home with her to make sure she did her part. She wanted to know if that would work for me because it had been a problem for her in the past with some of her coworkers. I told I was fine with that, but that I would make it clear in our next staff meeting this would be our arrangement going forward. She seemed to be surprised that I would make this known to everyone in the department because of the resistance I might encounter in the public forum of our staff meeting. I smiled and said, "We might as well talk about this in the open. It's not like people will miss the fact that you are leaving every day at 5:00 pm. What I want to make sure they *don't* miss is how early you're coming in or how much work you're taking home. My job is to work this out so you don't continue to have friction with your co-workers." How simple this all seems now, but looking back, it didn't seem that simple. It seemed like a huge hassle. Management Courage is always a hassle in the short-term — that's why so few people do it — but remember, it has huge benefits in the long-term. In this case, it ended some long-standing resentment that had been seething under the surface in the department for some time.

As long as we are on the subject of insidious inequities, look at how you treat your married employees versus your unmarried employees. Do you expect your single employees to work late and finish a project simply because they don't have a spouse calling to see why they are not home? Do you expect them to work most of the holidays because they're not married? Think about how acceptable this has become in corporate America.

How a Huge Mistake Taught Me the Value of Understanding *Individual* Employee Motivation

The real key to Principle Two is an understanding of what motivates each one of your employees. It is rarely the same thing from individual to individual. I failed to understand this until it smacked me in the face shortly after I joined a company as their Vice President of Human Resources.

The previous Vice President of Human Resources had been demoted rather than terminated. I took the job and arrived to find that everyone in the Human Resources Department hated me and loved her. I understood their need to blame me for what had happened to her. They all felt she'd gotten a raw deal. It didn't help that she was everybody's pal and they saw her as a surrogate mother.

The Commencement Address

My style couldn't have been any more different from hers. I decided the best way to deal with the situation was to try to keep everyone from transferring out of the department until they could get used to working for me and find out I was not a monster. So in my first staff meeting, I gave what I thought was my most motivating speech. It went something like this, "I know we've not worked together before, so I probably should tell you something about my management style. I'm a teacher by nature. I've got fifteen-plus years of human resources knowledge and I will teach you everything I know if you will stay to work with me. I'm sure all of you want to be a Vice President of Human Resources at some point in your career. If you stay to work for me, I'll get you ready for that big job you've always wanted. There are several other companies under our corporate umbrella that will need a head of Human Resources at some point in the future and I'll try to get you ready to run your own department so you will be a viable candidate when larger HR jobs open up." I thought it was an inspirational speech. And it *was* — for those motivated by the same things that motivate me. However, two of the people in that meeting came to tell me that they didn't want to be a Vice President of Human Resources and that they were going to begin looking at opportunities in other areas of the company so they *wouldn't* be forced to become a Vice President of Human Resources. My favorite was the person who told me, "I've seen the job. It's ugly and I don't want it!"

Boy, had I missed the mark with these two individuals

because I assumed everyone was motivated by career advancement. I took a step back and asked each one, "What attracted you to Human Resources? What do you like about the job?" in order to understand what motivated them. Both liked learning new things, but differed greatly in the things that interested them. We agreed that I would teach them some new things in the areas in which they were interested, but I had to swear I wouldn't try to make them a Vice President!

Further Insights into Individual Motivation

What motivates each person who works for you or with you? You are going to be asked this question at the end of the chapter. During an off-site strategic planning session for one of my clients, I made a group of sales managers list each person who worked for them, and put next to each person's name a sentence or phrase as to what motivated each one. Then I told them to look at what they had written. If any of the answers were the same, they were trying to force everyone into their own motivational template.

I saw my chances of doing any return work for this group plummet when one of the direct reports to the Senior Vice President of Sales turned to him and said, "I'd like to know what you wrote about each one of us." This really put the VP on the spot, but he showed remarkable Management Courage and read his first answer. It became obvious that the individual he was speaking about wasn't satisfied with his answer. I leapt in at this point and asked her, "Did he get it right, or would you adjust it a little?" She thought it needed adjustment and immediately told him what motivated her. She was the Director of Sales Administration and her job was to liaison with Accounting and Finance to get all deals approved. Her biggest motivation was for the sales team not to see her as the "bean counter" in the group, but to see her role as an integral part of the sales process and not treat her like she was a part of Finance or Accounting. The Sales VP went through his entire list and each person adjusted his thinking about what motivated him or her. To his credit, he took down everything they said, word for word, and changed his management style as he dealt with each one.

Perhaps the most enlightening moment for this group came when someone asked the VP what he thought motivated his Administrative Assistant, Catherine. Everyone liked Catherine, who was very smart and dedicated. She had been with us for the first part of the session, but had departed halfway through the session to go down to the boat they were using for the afternoon's entertainment in order to make sure everything was ready, including lunch. I knew this because she had stopped me before we started and told me she really was sorry to miss the second half of the session, but that she had to take care of lunch. I stopped the VP of Sales from answering the question about Catherine's motivation and asked the group what they thought it was since they all worked with her. I got various answers that ran along the line of appreciating her hard work. I surprised them by saying, "I'm not sure I agree with that. I'll tell you what I think and you decide if it's correct. I think the most important thing to

Catherine is not to be viewed as a secretary, but to be seen as a sales professional, too." Everyone thought about it and cited several examples of where they thought she'd made an effort to contribute as a sales person. Then I asked the tough question, "If that's her greatest motivator, why did you let her sit at the back of the room during the first half of the session, instead of at the U-shaped tables with the rest of you? And why is she not here for the second half of this session?" To their credit, they realized they'd been perfectly happy to treat her as a functionary when it was time to take care of their needs, and how unmotivating that must have been for her.

Manager's Mantra:

We must declare an end to "corporate egalitarianism."

Tom Rohrs, Senior Vice President of Applied Materials, Inc., was right when he railed against what he calls "corporate egalitarianism." He spoke about this in the context of across-the-board budget cuts. The gist of what he said was that organizations take 10% away from everybody instead of investing in what's critical. My favorite quote from him about this is, "There's too much democracy because no one wants to make anyone else unhappy."

Early in my career, I worked for a CEO who gave average annual bonuses to his five senior level executives. Each one got some sort of yearly in-kind bonus that was tailored to what brought him or her pleasure. One who liked to travel got an all-expenses-paid vacation. Another who liked cars got a very expensive sports car as a company car. When you'd done a particularly good job for the CEO, he looked for a reward that was personal to you. Money would have been easier, but much less impactful. I also came to understand that these rewards gave each person the chance to say repeatedly to others in their lives, "I did such a good job my boss gave me this." It was truly the gift that kept on giving, a tangible recognition of their efforts.

Whether you make a product, provide a service, are a for-profit or not-for-profit, public or private employer, your people are the competitive edge you have for moving your organization forward. Talent will be the greatest shortage facing employers in the future, and the ability to retain smart, hardworking individuals will be crucial for survival over the next few years. The only way to retain your talent is to tailor what you say and what you do to each individual you manage. It's easier to treat everyone the same, but managing with Management Courage is much more effective.

Unsettling Questions To Test Your Management Courage

1. How much do I know about each person I manage (or interact with on a regular basis) personally (non-work-related)? List each person and the things you know about him or her, such as family situation, what they like to do in their spare time, etc.

2. What is the biggest motivator for each person I manage (or interact with regularly)? (If you think the motivators are all the same, you are incorrect.)

3. When have I failed to recognize someone publicly because I thought it would offend another individual?

4. When have I failed to do something special for one of my better performers because I didn't want to be accused of favoritism?

NOTES

NOTES

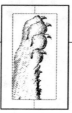

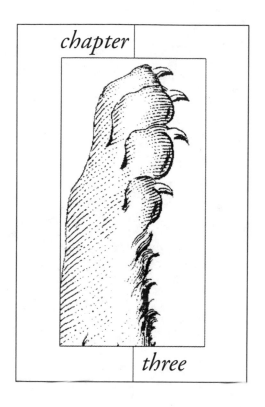

chapter

three

THE THIRD PRINCIPLE:
Don't Use Individuals or Policies As A Crutch

**"Management Courage prohibits using
individuals or policies as an excuse
or substitute for managing problems."**

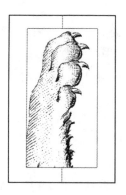

CHAPTER THREE

W E GIVE PEOPLE AUTHORITY, and develop policies, to bring order to the workplace. We do this so everyone knows how much vacation they can take, when to expect a performance review and what behavior is likely to get them terminated. As with all good intentions, we have corrupted these systems and used them to avoid dealing with problems. Employers institute policies and practices that allow them to wash their hands of resolving messy workplace problems. These include no-fault or point systems for attendance. We no longer have to discuss an employee's attendance problem with the employee. Instead, we add up the numbers, regardless of what caused the employee to be late or miss work, and let the total determine whether he or she stays or goes. This means some employees, who ride the system, stay much longer than they should and some long-term, wonderful employees, who have an unusual series of bad circumstances in a short period of time, find their jobs in jeopardy.

The same is true of the forced ranking systems that have become so popular. Instead of addressing managers who do not get rid of non-productive employees, we now have all managers rank their people from top to bottom and then lop off the lowest group in each department. This means that for managers who do an excellent job recruiting and developing good talent, we are getting rid of some really good people. It also means that, in the case of poor managers, we are keeping people who are dragging down the organization. We have invented a system that continues to allow managers not to step up to the plate. We say to some of the terminated employees, "Yes, I know how valuable you are, but someone has to be last and that's the system. I'm sorry I can't do anything about it. It's the policy." On top of that, we're letting some of them go regardless of whether we will have to replace them and train someone else who's probably not as good as they were! So, organizations shrug their shoulders and say, we can't get our managers to address this so we're going to use a system that forces them to do their job. We do this simply because we lack the Management Courage to hold managers accountable.

Manager's Mantra:

Never bury your head in "the policy."

I have designed and put into place performance review systems for a number of my clients. For any employee managing people, we add an additional section called

"Development of Subordinates." This usually causes an outcry when we roll it out among managers. They become indignant because we are holding them responsible for how well their people are doing. Well, who else should be held responsible? As managers, we are paid to develop people and address performance problems. That's the essence of management. If managers do this regularly, their employees either improve or eventually are terminated. If employees could do this on their own, we wouldn't need management!

As long as I'm attacking corporate sacred cows, I'll add several other policies or procedures to this Management Cowardice list. Per diems are an excellent example of not holding managers accountable. There isn't a single organization in America in which managers don't approve expense reports. Because managers are uncomfortable questioning expenses, we simply tell employees the maximum they can spend each day — and it's usually broken down by meal! It should be no surprise that almost all employees spend the maximum. So if you are working hard and skip lunch, we are going to penalize you for ordering a big dinner, even though economically our organization is better off. Even when we send employees to one of the 10 most expensive cities in the country, where our per diem is laughable, do we abandon the per diem that is not working and allow employees to use their own judgment? Absolutely not! We compound this lack of Management Courage by adding geographic differentials to the system. Managers need to look at expense reports and address expenses that are excessive, instead of making everyone adhere to a per diem because a few employees will take advantage.

Hiding Behind the
Performance Appraisal Policy

Many companies have given up training managers how to do effective performance appraisals and have purchased software that allows managers to point and click choices in each performance category and then print a neat, articulate performance review for each person they manage. It may keep managers from writing something embarrassing or illegal, but employees openly ask each other, "Did your manager give you the A, B, C, D, or E response in this category?" Employees' appraisals begin to look the same year after year because of this "cut and paste" method of managing the process and managers constantly ask why their employees don't seem motivated!

I once worked with a Senior Vice President of Sales who came to me at performance review time and explained to me that in the past, Human Resources had always given him someone to write his performance reviews because he was too busy. Apparently he would spend an hour going over each of his direct reports with the HR person and the HR person would "ghost write" his reviews. He was a Senior Vice President reviewing the five Vice Presidents who worked directly for him. I spent some time explaining to him how important an individualized performance review was to each employee, that it was one of the main factors in motivating employees to repeat good performance and address poor performance. Even more important, it set their direction for the coming year. When I finished, he still wanted one of my HR people to write the performance reviews, but now he wanted the best one at doing those "individualized performance appraisals." Luckily we both reported to the CEO and I told him he couldn't have any of my HR people, that he'd have to do his performance reviews this year. I was pleased to have put a stop to this practice until I heard from one of his direct reports that he'd had his Administrative Assistant do them for him. The big joke among his Vice Presidents was, "How did Connie rate your performance this year?"

Lay Off the Lame Excuses

I also include in this category of Management Cowardice mechanisms across-the-board budget reductions (See Tom Rohr's comments about these in Chapter 2) and software that determines who gets laid off when there is a reduction in force. Imagine how employees feel when they are told their manager really is sorry, but the computer picked them for lay-off!

If your lay-off policy only uses longevity as a criterion, your entire organization lacks Management Courage. (More heresy!) In a perfect world, your longest-term employees should be the most skilled, but that's not always the case. You should have a lay-off policy that begins with longevity, but also takes into account skill sets, performance reviews, corrective action in the past year, etc. It takes Management Courage to keep your best employees and face those who haven't worked very hard or kept up their skills and tell them why they were selected for lay-off. It also sends a message throughout your organization that those who work hard and learn new skills are earning job security.

I have spoken in this chapter about policies, procedures, and practices, but Management Courage also requires that you step up and be responsible for your own decisions — that you do not blame another manager for the course of action you've chosen. Nor do you blame them for inaction by saying, "I would do this for you, but So-and-So won't let me."

One of my most eye-opening experiences occurred when a manager came to see me about one of his employees. He said, "I'm going to tell you what one of my employees asked to do and I want you to say 'No.'" I was mystified until he explained that he didn't want to grant permission, but it would be easier on him if he could tell the employee he went to Human Resources and they said, "No." First, I had to get over my shock. Then I had to press the vein standing out on my head back into place. I told him I'd be glad to say "No" but was he sure he wanted to deliver that kind of unspoken message to his employees? He wanted to know what unspoken message I was talking about. "Well," I replied, "you're really telling your employees that I, not you, am running your department." He became indignant and said that wasn't true. I agreed with him, but pointed out that every time he told his employees he would do something, but Human Resources wouldn't let him, he was giving up his authority and telling the people who worked for him how powerless he was. He decided he would tell the employee "No" and send the clear message he was in charge.

Now you may think I manipulated him. I disagree. Because this *is* the unspoken message you send every time you don't take responsibility for your decisions. Your employees don't blame you, but they see you as weak, and many times will go over your head for help from someone whom they perceive as having real power in the organization. Managers chip away at their credibility when they do these kinds of things, and then are mystified as to why their people don't respect them.

Manager's Mantra:

Your employees will not always agree with your decisions, but they'll respect that they come from you — and that you *always* take responsibility.

When You Disagree with a Policy You're Supposed to Enforce

Several of the Management Courage questions at the end of this chapter ask what you do, as a manager, when you disagree with a policy, procedure, or practice. It is easy to disagree and be very vocal with your employees about it. This lets you off the hook as a manager, but is not Management Courage. Courageous managers challenge the status quo and don't pass the buck.

It takes Management Courage to take issue with a decision, or with the application of an organizational policy or procedure, but you should not discuss your disagreement with those you manage. You *should* talk to the people who can change the decision or make an exception based on an employee's particular situation, and you should do all you can to change the outcome. If you are unable to change the decision, then take responsibility and tell your employee "No." Don't blame others. You owe your employer loyalty, which includes being responsible for what happens to the employees you manage. In these types of situations, Management Courage requires that you disagree and then commit to the final decision, even when you don't personally support it.

Unsettling Questions To Test Your Management Courage

1. What individuals, policies, procedures, or practices do I, or others in our organization, routinely ignore or work around?

2. When have I told an employee I'd be willing to do something for him or her, but another individual in the organization would not permit it?

3. When have I enforced the standard policy, procedure, or practice rather than fashioning a specific solution for a unique situation?

4. When was the last time I disagreed with the results that came from adhering to a decision, policy, procedure, or practice? What did I do about it?

NOTES

NOTES

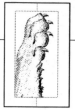

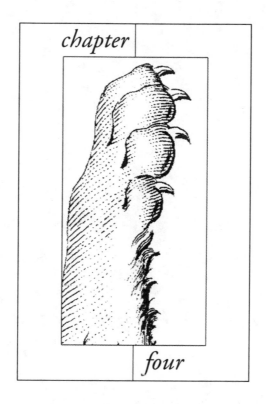

chapter

four

THE FOURTH PRINCIPLE:
Ask For and Give *Real* Feedback

"Management Courage requires that you seek
out accurate *negative* feedback about your
performance — and offer accurate, *gentle*
criticism to others about *their* performance."

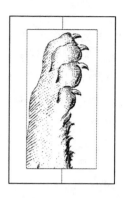

CHAPTER FOUR

W. SOMERSET MAUGHAM absolutely nailed it when he said, "People ask for criticism, but they only want praise." Nothing is more painful than criticism, but it forces you to grow if you seek it from wise people and heed it when you get it. Praise only makes you repeat what has worked in the past. Courageous managers challenge themselves by soliciting developmental feedback, rather than compliments.

When we ask our boss for feedback, most of us want to hear how well we're doing. It takes a great deal of Management Courage for people to give you negative feedback. You'll hate it and have to steel yourself for it. You'll also have a tendency to justify why you did something a certain way rather than listening to the feedback, or argue that a situation is not how the other person perceives it. This only causes the people giving the feedback to shut down and quit wasting their time. I know one manager who constantly says, "Feedback is a gift." I agree, but it is human nature to want to return an *ugly* gift.

Real feedback is very hard to come by in the workplace, especially if you are a higher-level individual in your organization. The higher up you are, the less you can trust feedback because people know there are consequences for disagreeing with or criticizing someone powerful and influential. So the next time someone tells you they like one of your projects or presentations, ask him or her, "What would I have to change or include for you to really *love* the project or presentation?" or, "What one thing would you change to make it even more effective?" You might try seeking out your greatest critic in the organization and asking for developmental suggestions.

A Meltdown that Brought Out True Management Courage

A manager once came to me shortly after one of his employees had a complete — and very loud — meltdown in the middle of his department. I became aware of the situation when I heard her screaming at him all the way down the hall. We sent her home and began to deal with the situation. Instead of being incensed, the manager said, "I never want that to happen again in my department. Can we go over what happened, so I can understand how to prevent this in the future?"

Now, this manager was quite good, and the employee had always been volatile. When I told him that, he repeated, "Can I go over everything that happened before Screamin' Mimi got so upset? And will you suggest other things I should have done to head this off or change the outcome?" He would not let himself off the hook. We reviewed all the circumstances to identify new strategies for handling this one employee, as well as ways to recognize when Screamin' Mimi was becoming unstable and to intervene as soon as possible to prevent another meltdown. Now, this doesn't mean we didn't address Screamin' Mimi's behavior as inappropriate, but the manager was more concerned with how to personally manage better, rather than how to address Screamin' Mimi's next outburst.

Manager's Mantra:

Courageous managers *encourage* disagreement and dissent.

Even more important, as the questions at the end of the chapter will suggest, what do you do with feedback once you have received it? If people spend valuable time offering you developmental suggestions and you don't change your behavior, why should they waste their time giving you more feedback in the future? If you ask for it, you must have the Management Courage to *do* something about it.

Courageous managers not only challenge themselves, they challenge those around them — *all the time.* They also accept being challenged by employees and see it as a growth opportunity because courageous managers do not equate disagreement with disloyalty. They foster an atmosphere that *encourages* disagreement and open dissent. When you have Management Courage, *no* subject should be undiscussable.

NASA experienced two horrific failures that can be traced to its culture of squelching disagreement and of "shooting the messenger." Both Space Shuttle disasters not only cost billions, but infinitely worse, they cost 14 human lives. After each accident, people from within came forward to say they knew there were problems, but were afraid to speak up. Along with reviewing what went wrong technically, NASA began to work with outside consultants to remake its culture and allow people to disagree with their bosses without fear of losing their jobs or ruining their careers.

One of the advantages of being a consultant is I'm in and out of 15 organizations per month and meet a lot of managers. I can't tell you how often I've heard a manager say, "I have an open door policy. My people can come tell me anything." I could retire tomorrow if I had a dollar for every time I've seen employees roll their eyes after a manager said that. There are very few managers who actually practice an effective open door policy.

A Novel Way to Share Bad News

When I was fresh out of college, I had the opportunity to work for a CEO who was truly an entrepreneur before business people even began using that word. He was a self-made millionaire by age 35. He was one of the smartest people for whom I have worked, and one of the scariest. He was famous for screaming at people who brought bad news or made mistakes.

I once had bad news I needed to share with him and it

took me two days to screw up the courage to go see him. I shared my dilemma with a few of my co-workers, who only kept saying in a very dirge-like tone, "Oh, Margaret!" As a matter of fact, an unofficial pool began betting on whether I'd still have a job when I left his office. My only hope of surviving was if I could make him laugh, because he *did* have a good sense of humor. I finally knocked on his door and was admitted to the inner sanctum with a gruff, "Come in." When Bruce Bannister looked up from his work, he told me to have a seat. He then said he'd be with me in a minute and went back to work.

About three minutes later, he finished and looked up to find me bent at the waist, scrunched up in the fetal position in the chair in front of his desk. He demanded, "What are you doing?"

I didn't even look up, but said, "I'm ready."

Impatiently he asked, "Ready for what?"

"I'm ready to be shot," I replied.

Growing more exasperated, his volume rising, he demanded, "What the h*** are you talking about?" (I'm sure the odds in the pool were going up against me exponentially at this point!)

I said, "I'm ready to be shot. Everyone says you always shoot the messenger who brings bad news." I think he was both startled and amused that I had the guts to say this to his face. I wish I could tell you it was Management Courage, but it was simply survival. I figured he was going to fire me any way.

He got quiet and said, "I suppose that means you have bad news."

I nodded my head, still in the fetal position, and said,

"Yes sir, Mr. Bannister. It's pretty bad. As a matter of fact, there's a pool going to see how long it takes you to fire me."

"Then I guess you'd better sit up, tell me, and get it over with," he said. At that point, I straightened up, looked him in the eye and told him.

He settled back and said, "That's not so bad. Is there anything else?"

"No sir!" I replied.

"Then get back to work and straighten this out!" he said. As I got up to leave, he added, "And tell everyone, I didn't shoot you."

To which I replied, "Yes sir, I will, but they won't believe it!" and left his office.

Even if you don't see employees crouched in the fetal position, you should realize many employees work for managers who emotionally put them there.

Manager's Mantra:

Courageous managers offer a *balance* of positive and negative feedback. The negative feedback is *gentle* criticism that helps people grow and develop.

Using Principle Four to Overcome Negative Peer Ratings

One of the hardest pieces of feedback I ever got came in a 360-degree feedback project done with the six top managers in my company. My ratings from the CEO, and from the people who worked for me, were excellent. My ratings from my peers also were fine. But one issue that surfaced was they felt I was not trustworthy. I found this devastating, because I pride myself on keeping my word and doing what I say I will. I also believed strongly in personal ethics. My peer group was not the easiest group with whom to work, and it would have been easy to chalk this up to my being the only woman in Senior Management or to my being responsible for enforcing policies they didn't like.

Finally, I got a hold of myself and decided to quit rationalizing why their feedback wasn't valid. I went to see all my peers and told them this clearly was an issue, and that I wanted to understand this so I could work on it.

At first, each one denied saying it, but I pushed and said, "It's clear from the tight range of responses that everyone in my peer group believes this, and I want to change it. I cannot change what I don't understand. I need your help in giving me examples of times in which you believe I wasn't trustworthy."

None of my peers would offer an example involving themselves, but they mentioned examples others had shared with them. I finally understood that they had never worked in an environment in which the head of Human Resources reported directly to the CEO. They were used to Human Resources coming to them when there was a problem in their area, whereas I was going straight to the CEO, as he expected, in order to report problems. They then would find out there was an issue when the CEO talked to them, either with or without me present. After I understood this, I could clearly imagine how "shanghaied" they felt when this happened. So

I started changing how I dealt with the people issues that arose in their areas. I would consult with them first to work out how we were going to handle it. *Then* I would go to the CEO, often asking them to go with me. The following year, when we conducted 360-degree feedback again, my peer ratings were excellent and the trustworthiness problem had disappeared.

It would have been much easier — and less painful — to do nothing, to tell myself I was just doing my job, as the CEO wanted me to. It would have been cowardly, and much less effective, to ignore the feedback and not deal with it.

Unsettling Questions To Test Your Management Courage

1. When was the last time I got negative feedback on my performance?

2. How did I respond to the negative feedback?

3. What have I changed about my behavior as a result of that negative feedback?

4. When was the last time someone told me they liked my work?

5. Did I push them for suggestions as to how to *improve* the work?

6. When was the last time I gave someone else a piece of negative feedback? How would I have felt if someone had said the same thing to me?

NOTES

NOTES

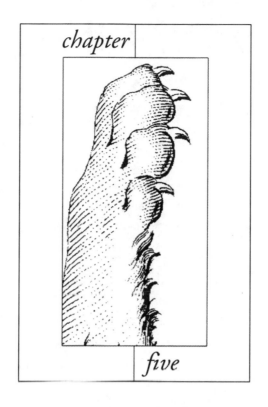

chapter

five

THE FIFTH PRINCIPLE:
Take the Blame

**"Management Courage requires taking
responsibility for any mistakes I — or
the people who work for me — make."**

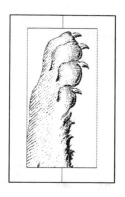

CHAPTER FIVE

I N THIS WORLD OF POLITICAL SPIN and legal defenses we never had 10 years ago, very few people take responsibility for their own actions, much less the actions of anyone else. Managers complain constantly about the lack of loyalty on the part of employees, but cannot recall the last time they took the blame for one of their employees' mistakes. We are constantly asking employees to take risks and yet don't cover for employees when those risks have negative results.

Most organizations have to try five new ideas to get one that works. They will be sadly lacking in new ideas if the careers of four people end each time they try five new ideas, but that is what happens in organizations today.

Manager's Mantra:

Never make employees suffer for a bad decision they have made. They will quit taking chances and trying new things.

Wernher von Braun, the scientist who helped America develop its rocket program, once sent a bottle of champagne to an engineer on his team who confessed he might have inadvertently short-circuited a missile during a critical test. The engineer saved the team days of expensive redesign because of his confession. Ben and Jerry's Ice Cream used to throw periodic parties to celebrate mistakes because the founders believed people would take bigger risks if they weren't penalized for failing.

A successful consultant I know told me the best manager he ever had was one he had in college when he worked as an electrician's helper. He told me two things George (his best manager) had to say about making mistakes. The first was, "As long as you're messin' up, I know you're staying busy." The second was, "I don't mind you shooting yourself in the foot once in a while, just stop reloading." These two attitudes made George the best manager in this consultant's 25-year career.

This is the hardest of the Management Courage principles for me. When I am asked about the most courageous thing I've done in my career, I think of two moments in particular. The first situation was a horrible failure of Management Courage on my part, but it set me up to do better in the second situation.

Before I go into detail, let me offer some background and context.

Every time I am fortunate enough to lead a group of people, I tell them there are two things that will get them fired: breaking confidentiality and lying. I manage by telling those in my department everything I can about what is going on in the organization, even at the highest levels, so they can make good decisions. This only works if they never discuss these things outside our department, making confidentiality the backbone of our group.

Similarly, I believe everything my employees tell me and use their information to make decisions. I consider a guess a lie, if it's presented as the truth, just as I consider covering up a mistake to be the worst of all lies. If you don't know something, tell me you don't know, and then go find out. If you make a mistake, tell me and we will fix it.

Behind my back this became known as "The Talk." I only became aware of its effectiveness when people in the department insisted I interview someone we were adding to the department, but who would not be reporting to me. When I assured them I trusted their judgment, they insisted I interview this person, wanting to make sure all new people got "The Talk" because it was the way we functioned as a work group.

The first few times people came to me, they were quick to remind me I had said there was no mistake that couldn't be corrected as long as they told me about it. This preface worked well for me, because it gave me an opportunity to compose myself for what was coming next. I would then discuss with them what we needed to do to fix the situation. As the people I worked with became more confident there really wasn't a penalty for making a mistake, the preface disappeared and they would come into my office and say, "I really screwed up."

Now for my dismal failure at Principle Five. One day, one of the people I worked with came into my office. Giving no preface or preamble, she told me about a huge mistake she had made. I was unprepared and mishandled the whole situation. I gasped and said, "That *is* a huge mistake. How could you have done that?" She looked like I'd hit her — and rightfully so. I had to back up and apologize on the spot for what I'd said and then asked her to tell me how it happened.

I was so distraught over how I'd mishandled the situation, I was determined never to do that again. It was probably what stiffened my spine for the scariest moment of Management Courage in my career. I joined a company as their Vice President of Human Resources. I was reporting directly to the CEO, who in turn reported directly to Hollerin Harry, the Chairman of the Board of our parent company. During the interview process, I asked the question all of us ask at some point, "How does this position come to be open?" (Translation: What happened to the last person in this job?)

That would be Susie. It seems Susie had miraculously decided the job was too much for her, and she chose to take a step back to work for whoever would be the new Vice President of Human Resources. When I asked how Susie felt about this step backward, I was assured that she was fine with it. Of course, I arrived for my first day of work to find she was *not* fine — and neither was anyone else in the department, all of whom had worked for Susie for years and felt great loyalty to her.

Shortly after I joined the company, we had to do several waves of lay-offs due to a huge, recent acquisition. A few people had been laid off in the months prior and had been given additional benefits as part of their severance package. When we had to do the next lay-off of 25 people, my CEO and Hollerin' Harry told me they had run the cost of the additional benefits for the 300 or so people they anticipated would be laid off over the next year, and could not afford to offer those additional benefits as a part of severance packages. I assigned Susie to put together the severance packages for the next round of lay-offs and instructed her to remove the additional benefits from the severance packages.

I received a call from Payroll stating they were not going to cut severance checks for the 25 people who had been laid off because we had offered them additional benefits we were not authorized to offer. I had to tell the CEO we had inadvertently offered this group the old severance package. He notified Hollerin' Harry. I, in turn, received a phone call from Hollerin Harry I could hold at arms length and still hear, asking me if I understood the new severance package. I assured him I did and that I would correct it for future lay-offs. I then went to Susie's office to ask how this had happened. She told me, "I don't know. I must have had some old documents in my system that got printed out by mistake." I had Susie call up all the documents she had in her system and watched her delete the portion of the documents that granted additional benefits beyond the new severance policy.

Our next lay-off was about 75 people. I got *another* call from Payroll informing me they would not issue severance checks because we were still offering the additional benefits. These additional benefits represented a huge monetary obligation for the company. When I went down to tell my CEO, he was horrified and speechless. Thirty minutes later, he called me to his office where I found Hollerin' Harry. I steeled myself for the dressing down I was going to get, when my CEO said, "Tell Hollerin' Harry what you told me." That's when I realized that my CEO lacked the Management Courage to even tell his boss what had happened and was leaving it up to me. I told Hollerin Harry and he became apoplectic. He got right up in my face and started yelling at me, demanding to know who on my staff was responsible for the paperwork on these layoffs. As I stared at the pulsing vein in his forehead, I told him it didn't matter who was responsible, that I, as the head of Human Resources, was ultimately responsible. At that, Hollerin' Harry told me I *was* going to tell him who did the paperwork. By this point, he was about three inches from my face and spitting on me he was so angry. I drew a deep breath and remembered what a disappointment I'd been the last time I needed to shield one of the people who worked with me. I said, "No sir. I'm not going to tell you. I'm the Vice President of Human Resources. It happened on my watch and I am ultimately responsible. Why don't I tell you what I'm going to do in the future to ensure this never occurs again?" I then went on to explain that no matter how many lay-offs we had to do in the future, I would personally check every severance package. Since we anticipated about 200, this was going to be an arduous task. Hollerin' Harry's sense of fairness would not let him punish me for something I hadn't directly done, but he made it clear that any additional mistakes in the severance packages would result in my termination *without* a severance package.

Needless to say, I had to get a grip on myself before I went to see Susie. I composed myself, went to her office, closed the door and said, "I have taken the last chewing out for you I am going to take. This was not an error, it was sabotage. For this reason, nothing can be sent out by you that I don't check. When I check it, I will initial it. If any of your documents leave this office without my initials, I will fire you. I no longer trust you. If you want to remain here long-term, you need to decide how you will earn my trust back." (See Principle One about honesty.)

While the whole experience was very stressful, I got a huge benefit from it. Everyone had heard the exchange between Hollerin' Harry and me. Everybody knew Susie had sabotaged me and that I refused to offer her up as a scapegoat even when I wanted her gone. It earned me instant loyalty from the people who had worked for, and with, Susie. They began to offer ideas and suggestions, rather than just grudgingly administer my ideas.

Manager's Mantra:

Employees will dare greater things if they know they work for a manager who will take a bullet for them.

Managers need to discuss each mistake as it's made so everyone can learn from it and make better decisions next time. This also helps employees become adept at assessing risks. (See the previous chapter on feedback.) Managers have to strike the balance between empowering and enabling… much like George did with his two statements. Management Courage makes a post-mortem a regular part of any project that isn't going well.

Courageous managers ask the following questions in a manner that clearly communicates they are looking to learn, not to locate a scapegoat:

• What seems to be wrong with the project or situation?

• Should we continue this course of action?

• How can we anticipate these problems in the future?

• What should we do differently in the future to make sure this doesn't happen again?

To test what kind of shield you are for people, see how many CYA (cover your a**) memos people send you. If you are getting any, this is a sign that the writer doesn't trust you to step up when things go wrong, or that you are the kind of manager who places blame when things get tough. Otherwise, why would anyone take time in his or her busy schedules to compose the memo?

Finally, you are not taking the blame or shielding someone if you cover for them and then tell everyone about it. That's not Management Courage. It is only courageous if you cover their mistake or error and do not tell anyone about it. Never make another person's mistake public. If it becomes public, assume responsibility for the error and then discuss it with the individual one-on-one in private.

Unsettling Questions To Test Your Management Courage

1. When was the last time I publicly admitted making a mistake?

2. When was the last time any one admitted to me they had made a mistake? What was my reaction? Whom have I told about the mistake?

3. When was the last time I took responsibility for someone else's mistake?

4. When was the last time I covered for someone without telling anyone?

5. Who in my organization is sending me CYA memos? What do I need to do to earn their trust?

6. Am I making the same kinds of decisions today I was making a year ago? This indicates the people with whom I work are not stepping up to make decisions. What is it about my management style that is preventing them from doing so?

7. What was the last project and/or initiative on which I did a post-mortem?

NOTES

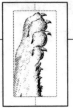

NOTES

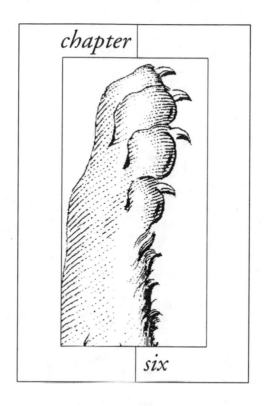

chapter

six

THE SIXTH PRINCIPLE:
Leave Soul-Sucking Situations

**"Management Courage is changing jobs
when the culture or position is not
a good fit or is contrary to your values
or personal code of ethics."**

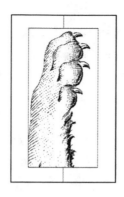

CHAPTER SIX

W E SPEND WAY TOO MUCH TIME working to have it draw the life out of us. Marti Smyth, a career consultant and author of the book *Is It Too Late to Run Away and Join the Circus?*, says only about 10% of all the people who think about making a career change actually do it, and that most of those are forced into the change because they get fired or because their employer moves away.

When I talk about a disconnect between your personal values and your job, I'm not talking about the usual job hassles we all face. I'm talking about a job that makes you miserable over an extended period of time. For example, your job keeps you traveling four days per week. You loved it when you started, but now you are married with a new baby and want to be home at night. You're making a lot of money, but if you quit traveling, your employer has no other place for you.

I went to law school when I was 25, expecting to do truth, justice, and the American way. A few weeks of law school cured me of that. I became a trial lawyer and practiced for about four years. I loved to win, but I hated everything else about practicing law. The most rewarding case I ever won was one in which I spent 10 to 15 hours working for a court-awarded fee of one hour of my time. I made a dishonest appliance dealer take back a defective, second-hand appliance he had sold an elderly couple, despite his posted signs stating "No returns."

As the years went by, I found myself wishing my clients would never need me again, which is contrary to building a successful law practice. I needed to be part of a team and to build something. I finally got out of law, despite three years of law school, passing the bar exam, and four years of practice. I went back to Human Resources, which is what I had done before law school.

Everyone told me I had wasted seven or eight years of my life. The next job I went to ended five months after I took it and I was out of work for more than nine months after that. Everyone thought I'd made a mistake and kept encouraging me to return to practicing law. I finally landed a great job heading Human Resources for a large manufacturing company. The CEO who interviewed me told me he hired me because I sold him on the fact that he was getting two for the price of one with me — someone to manage Human Resources *plus* a lawyer who would help reduce legal expenses.

It takes real bravery to say I need more satisfaction out of my life, not more money.

Manager's Mantra:

Make sure what you *do* is in line with who you *are*.

Make a list of the five to seven most fulfilling moments in your life. What do they tell you about the values that drive your life? Then make a list of the five to seven most fulfilling moments in your current job or profession. Do both lists contain the same types of experiences? If not, what you *do* is not in line with who you *are*. Can you reconfigure your job so it offers more fulfillment? If not, have the Management Courage to find a new career. If you can't find five fulfilling moments in your current job . . . well, it's long past time to change what you do. Forget about how many people caution against it. They are not slogging to your job every day. It takes Management Courage to choose a different career when everyone counsels you to stay where you are.

Now for the other half of soul-sucking work. What if you love your job, but the person or organization you work for does not have the same value system you have? The good news is you don't have to change careers. The bad news is you do have to find someone else for whom to do your job.

I'm not talking about a small disagreement about how things should be done. Your boss and/or organization will always make decisions with which you will not be happy. This disagreement has to be a major philosophical schism between your values or ethics system and that of the organization and/or person for whom you work. This difference should be based on the actual actions of your manager or organization regarding what is allowed to go on, not what management *decrees* is acceptable behavior. In most organizations, there is a huge chasm between the mission statement and what actually takes place.

Enron had a lengthy ethics manual, which laid out what was acceptable behavior. People read it, but several senior members of management didn't adhere to it and suffered no penalty for not following the ethics code. To this day, people still wonder why employees didn't leave the company or report the behavior. Any honest human being should understand it. Employees were making a lot of money; their 401(k)s were increasing in value exponentially. Enron was the darling of the corporate world and they were working with other people they liked. Who'd want to quit that or be ostracized and/or fired for reporting unethical or illegal conduct? The life of a whistleblower is very lonely and not usually profitable, despite the newspaper stories.

It takes even more Management Courage to leave these types of situations than to make a career change. You love what you doing, so why should you leave to do the same job somewhere else, where you will have to start over and probably make less money? Because the "soul toll" for these types of situations is huge.

I once had a job I loved, working with a team that took me five years to put together. We were doing some wonderful things and the work was exciting and cutting-edge. Then senior management changed and I wound up reporting to Mr. Slither, a person whose ethics were not the same as mine.

Mr. Slither made it known, when we were looking for a third-party vendor to service a particular employee benefit, that the vendor who wined and dined him the most would get the business. There was an absolute disregard for what kind of service the vendor would give our employees.

I called the vendor I believed would offer our employees the best service and leveled with them. They immediately asked if they could take Mr. Slither, the Benefits Manager, and me to dinner. They flew in several of their executives for the dinner at the restaurant of our choice. Mr. Slither chose one of the most expensive restaurants in town and brought Mrs. Slither. Once he made it known he was bringing his spouse, the Benefits Manager and I were invited to bring a guest, but we politely declined. There were 10 people at dinner that night and the Slithers ordered everything from appetizers to expensive port at the end of the meal. The vendor got the business, but I found myself ashamed to have taken part in the process.

It became especially clear to me how much of a toll these work situations take on us several months after I left the job. I was having my teeth cleaned and my dentist said out of the blue, "You must have made a major change in your life." I was startled and said, "Yes, I changed jobs." To which he immediately replied, "Whatever you do, don't go back." When I asked how he knew I'd made a major change, he told me he'd noticed over the last year or two my gums were getting paler and paler with each visit, a sure sign of increased stress. Now they were healthy and pink like they should be. While I'm loath to discuss dental health in a business book, I cannot imagine the invisible damage we do to ourselves when we stay and work for people (or in situations) that are leeching the very health out of us. We wouldn't want to work unprotected in a situation that was physically toxic to us, but we stay in situations that are mentally and emotionally poisonous to us because the money is good and the damage is not immediately visible.

Manager's Mantra:

**Choose work that enhances your life,
not that merely funds your existence.**

It takes Management Courage to leave lucrative situations that are vexatious to your spirit, yet the price we pay is much higher than the wages we earn.

Unsettling Questions To Test Your Management Courage

1. Make a list of the five to seven most fulfilling moments in your life. What do they tell me about the values that drive my life?

2. Make a list of the five to seven most fulfilling moments in your current job. Do both lists contain the same types of experiences?

3. How can I reconfigure my current job so that it offers more fulfillment?

4. What are the areas in which my boss (or organization) and I disagree? Are these style differences, or are they issues about dishonest or unethical treatment of employees, the public, or shareholders?

5. Does my current employer have policies, procedures, or practices with which I disagree vehemently? Are these moral or ethical issues?

6. Is my current employer and/or work situation in line with my personal code of ethics and behavior?

NOTES

NOTES

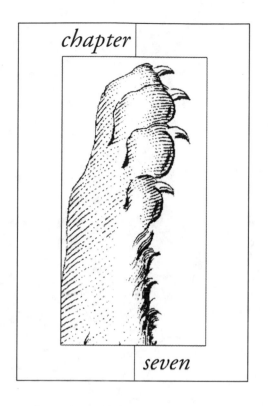

chapter

seven

MANAGE
COURAGEOUSLY

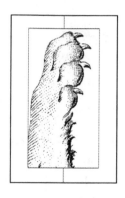

CHAPTER SEVEN

W HEN I SPEAK on the topic of Management Courage, I am always asked how someone can determine what the correct Management Courage choice is in any situation. That's easy. You look at all the options available to resolve the situation. The Management Courage choice is always the one that is the hardest for you personally, makes you the most uncomfortable, and causes you the most pain for the longest period of time.

These days most people yearn for healthy work environments and meaningful work. Several recent polls report that at least 50% of the people in the workforce today are not satisfied with their current job. In other words, at least half the people working dislike their current job, and many of them actually *hate* their jobs. Trends indicate this number will continue to rise. With many of the Baby Boomers retiring over the next few years, great employees will suddenly have far more job opportunities to consider. With that many offers, employees will make different choices in the future. They will become more particular about the organizations and individuals with which they will be willing to work. Management Courage will become one of the ways rare managers set themselves apart. What smart employees wouldn't want a manager who is honest, treats them like the unique individuals they are, never makes excuses, encourages them to take risks, protects them when things don't work out, and wants them to be happy?

While I know it is easy to talk about Management Courage and hard to display it, I encourage you to work through the questions at the end of each chapter to get a realistic view of where you are in this metamorphosis. The questions will show you the areas where you need to begin working. I challenge you to do one Management Courage act per week in your workplace. If you do this, Management Courage will become a regular part of your work. You will dramatically raise your job satisfaction level — as well as that of those who work with and for you.

NOTES

NOTES

NOTES

ABOUT
MARGARET MORFORD

MARGARET MORFORD is President of *The HR Edge, Inc.*, a national management consulting and training company. She is often quoted as a management/workplace expert by America's top newspapers, including *The Wall Street Journal*, *USA Today*, and the *Chicago Tribune*. She appears regularly on ABC, CBS, and Fox-TV affiliates. She twice has been rated one of the top five speakers at the Society for Human Resource Management national conference (2004 and 2005). She also is the host and author of the nationally-distributed video *Running with the Big Dogs: How to Make HR a Strategic Player*.

Her clients have included Lockheed Martin, Chevron, Time Warner, Sara Lee Foods, Home and Garden Television, Deloitte, Allied Insurance, NAPA Auto Parts, New York Presbyterian Hospital (Cornell & Columbia Medical Centers), U.S. Marine Corps, Blue Cross Blue Shield, Fox Broadcasting, Schwarz Biosciences, Northwestern Mutual

Life Insurance Company, SAS (computer software), The Nashville Predators hockey franchise, The Peabody Hotel, The Hartford, AmSurg, Quorum Health Resources, U.S. Naval Nuclear Submarine Group, and various local and state governments.

Prior to owning her own company, Ms. Morford was Sr. Vice President, Human Resources Consulting, for a national consulting firm out of Winston-Salem, North Carolina. She has served as Vice President of Human Resources for three large companies. She has a BS degree from the University of Alabama and a JD degree from the Vanderbilt University School of Law. She also has worked as an attorney, specializing in employment law.

Margaret Morford offers seminars, workshops, presentations, and speeches to organizations and business groups across the U.S.

For more information, please visit www.thehredge.net.

Printed in the United States
139738LV00003BA/3/A

9 781583 850893